Mixed emotions

Laurence Guerrier

BookLeaf Publishing

Presentation by *BookLeaf Publishing*

Web: www.bookleafpub.com

E-mail: info@bookleafpub.com

ISBN: 978-93-95755-36-8

First edition 2022

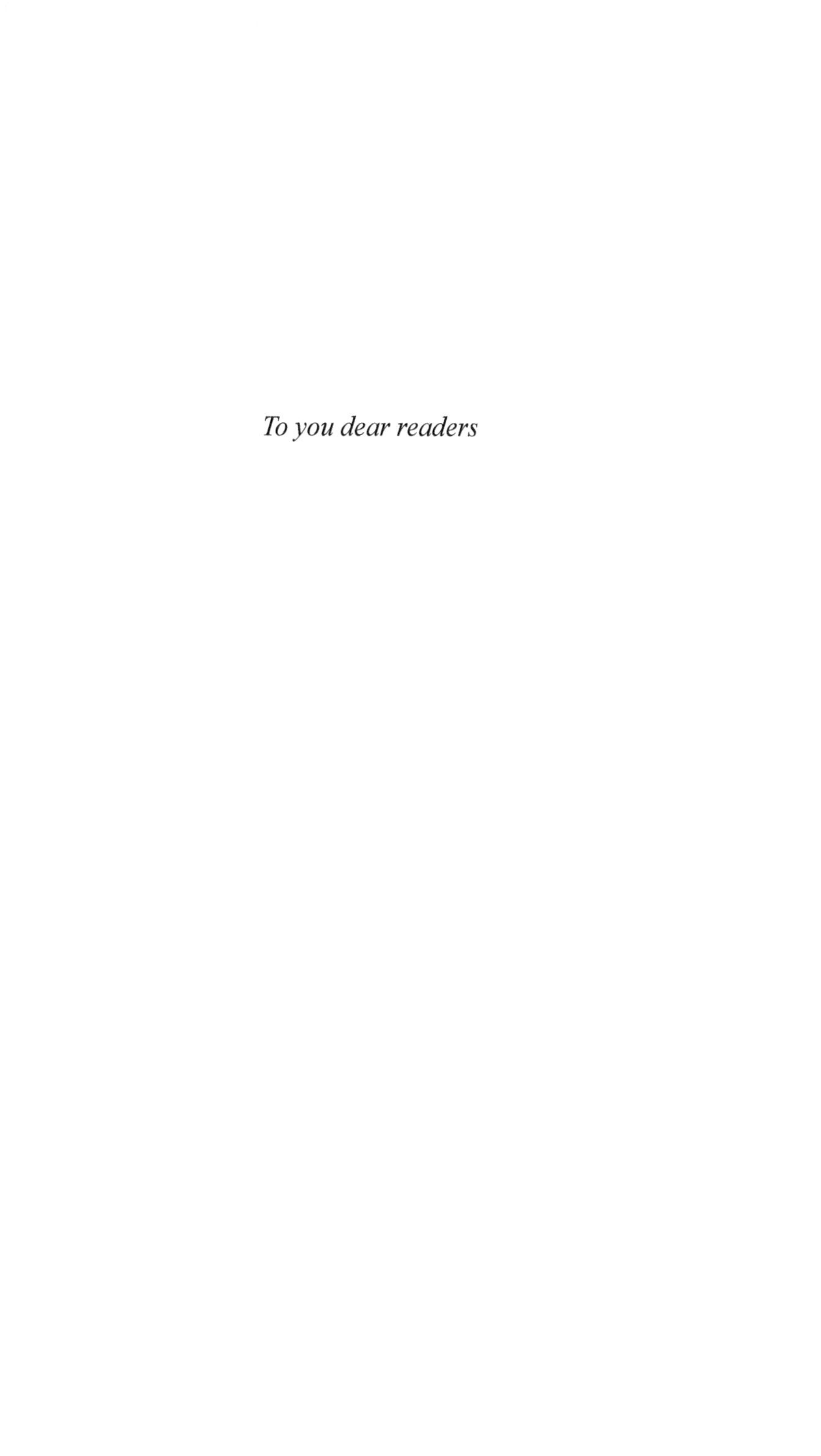

To you dear readers

Illusion

She thought that everything was perfect,
She thought that she could overcome it
But if I'm honest with you,
She couldn't

The pain she suffered wasn't new,
She felt that way for a long time.
Too long
It has become who she is
Took all that was left of her

Her happiness, her joy, her smile,
Everything, it all went away,
The pain took it all
Suffocating her.

She wanted to be set free,
To feel those incredible feelings,
But the pain speaks louder,
She's imprisoned in her own body
She can't get away,
She won't get away.

Why didn't you do anything

You looked at her,
Saw the pain she went through,
But decided it wasn't good enough for you
To help her feel better.

You looked at her
While she was crying,
Slowly dying
But couldn't make her feel better.

Do you remember
When she was there for you?
When she answered her phone at 3 in the
morning
Only to make you feel better?

Do you remember
When she helped you?
Please tell me you do !
Please tell me

Why couldn't you help her?
Why couldn't you at least try?
Why did you let her die?

My body

My body wasn't yours to take
My body wasn't yours to use
For your pleasure
My body wasn't yours to destroy
To take advantage of,
My body was supposed to be mine.
MINE ONLY.

But you decided to
Destroy it

I am trying to put back the pieces together
Pieces that shouldn't have been broken
If you'd listen to my screaming « no's!»
Pieces that shouldn't have been lost
If you'd listen when I told you
« I don't want this !»
Pieces that shouldn't be so difficult to find
If you'd understood when I pushed you away,
When I started crying,
When I screamed
When I beg
For you to stop it.
Those pieces shouldn't be that hard to glue back
together
If you'd understood

That I didn't want it.

In pain

From the pain you caused me,
My body is in agony.
I didn't ask you to
Tear me into pieces,
To take what wasn't yours.
I didn't ask you to ruin me,
But entitled as you are,
You decided to hurt me the best you could.

Remember

Do you remember a time
When everything was perfect?
When everything felt good?
I remember that time,
It was easy, easier before I met you

Do you remember that time,
When I gave you my heart?
My love? My whole life?
Do you remember? Tell me

Do you remember when I was there,
Morning and night doesn't matter 'cause
I was there,
I cared about you, loved you,
You didn't,
But I was still there.

I remember you
Crashing, tossing, stepping, throwing
My heart, torture it, breaking it,
I do remember
The wholes you draw on my soul,
The pain, the sadness you make me
Go through

I remember you
Talking behind my back,
Spreading lies, use my kindness
And came back all smile,

I remember you
Trusting him over me
Letting him take advantage of
My body.
I remember you

Truth

Truth is, she's lost
In her thoughts
Always thinking
Of what could happen
And what could not.

Truth is, she doesn't know
How to feel anymore
Cause each time,
It felt wrong and unnatural.

Truth is, she's burning
from the inside,
Like a volcano that could
Irrupt at any time.

Truth is, she's hurting
Deeply inside.
In her own thoughts,
She's slowly drowning
It is only a matter of time.

No more regrets

I regret loving you,
Caring so much about you
That I forgot how to
Love and care
About myself.

I regret putting you first
Putting your needs
Before mines

I regret all those moments
I spent with you
Has you only brought me
Temporary happiness

But,
I don't regret letting you go.
Getting rid of your toxic character.

Forgiving you

See, for what seems like an eternity
A storm of emotion consumed my entire body
A hurricane took place,
Tearing apart everything on its way
Without any mercy
Without any warning.
It just happened.
It's uncontrollable.

I want to stop it,
I need to stop it.
But, for that,
I need to do the impossible,
I need to forgive you.
Forgive those wrongful actions.
Forgive all that emotional
Manipulation.

I need to forgive you.
For my good,
For my sanity
Not for you
But for
Me.

Unrecognizable

I am standing there,
In front of my mirror
Unable to recognize
The girl.
The sad girl
That is standing
In front of me.

Myself

I genuinely don't care anymore
If you want to be a part of my life or not.
I'm done waiting,
I'm done putting myself on hold,
I'm done giving you all my energy,
I choose myself over you
And that's the best feeling ever.

Wasted time

I do not regret losing you
I only regret the time I wasted
With you.

Letting you go

I have to let you go,
Let go of the beautiful memories we had
together,
Let go of our habits,
Let go of every single moment we spent
Laughing, Crying, Loving
Singing out loud, Cooking, Camping
Stargazing, Traveling
Living,
I have to let go of an entire life
And I have absolutely no idea how to do it.

One last time

Take me in your arms, one last time.
Tell me how much you loved me, one last time.
Whisper loving words in my ears, one last time.
Kiss me, one last time.
Love me, one last time.
I beg you, smile at me one last time.
Before you go
Before letting me feel this emptiness
Inside my chest.
Just one last time.

Pain

She thought that everything was perfect,
She thought that she could overcome it.
But if I'm honest with you,
She couldn't.

The pain she suffered wasn't new.
She felt that way for a long time.
Too long
It has become who she is
Took all that was left of her.

Her happiness, her joy, her smile,
Everything, it all went away.
The pain took it all
Suffocating her.

She wanted to be set free,
To feel those incredible feelings,
But the pain speaks louder,
She's imprisoned in her own body
She can't get away,
She won't get away.

Missing you

I miss your minty smell
That I took pleasure in inhaling when you were
hugging me.
I miss the growing warmth in my heart,
When you were smiling at me.
I miss the feeling of your lips against mine
When you were slowly kissing me.
I miss that spark in my eyes
When you were texting me.

I miss you.

Lost

When you left,
I was devastated,
I never thought I'd be so attached to you,
Never thought I'd be addicted to your laugh,
Never thought I'd be craving for your touch,
But I was.

I wanted you here, with me,
Your arms around my body,
Your lips near my ear,
Whispering happy souvenirs.

I wanted to see you smile,
Your big bright smile,
Your brown eyes,
That used to give me butterflies.

But you're nowhere to be found,
And i'm desperately crying on the ground.

Don't care

I genuinely don't care anymore
If you want to be a part of my life or not.
I'm done waiting,
I'm done putting myself on hold,
I'm done giving you all my energy,
I choose myself over you
And that's the best feeling ever.

Tell me what you see

Close your eyes,
Tell me do you hear my voice shaking?
Do you hear the soreness of it?

Open your eyes now,
Look at me,
Tell me, do you see the pain in my eyes?
Do you see the tears forming in the corner?

I've been holding on so much,
I was keeping this pain to myself

All those smiles, the excitement you saw before

They were all lies.

I thought

We had a perfect moment
We had a perfect relationship
Together we were good
Or that's what I thought.

Did you enjoyed it

Did you enjoy it?
Enjoy seeing me cry,
Enjoy seeing me scream,
Enjoy seeing me lose my mind ?

Tell me, did you enjoy it ?
Seeing me closing my eyes,
Seeing me slowly giving in
Seeing me succumbing to the pain?

Did you truly enjoy it ?

Haunting

Trust me,
I am trying to heal
But I can't seem to let it go.
This event,
Is constantly playing in my head.
Haunting me
Day and Night
How long do I have to live with this pain?

You'll get better soon

We are all hurting in someways
Some mastered the art of hiding their pain
Others find a way to ignore it.
Others let it consume them.
Either way,
No matter how you deal with it,
I hope you'll get better soon.

Take care!